To:

From:

If I Knew Then
What I Know Now...

MICHAEL W. DOMIS

PETER PAUPER PRESS, INC.
White Plains, New York

To my son, Sean
I'm proud of you every day.

Designed by Taryn R. Sefecka

Photo credits appear on pages 86-87

Copyright © 2003
Peter Pauper Press, Inc.
202 Mamaroneck Avenue
White Plains, NY 10601
All rights reserved
ISBN 0-88088-324-3
Printed in China
7 6 5 4 3 2

Visit us at www.peterpauper.com

If I Knew Then
What I Know Now...

INTRODUCTION

Oh! If I knew then what I know now, I would never have made a mistake, or at least not as many. I would have done some things differently. Or, maybe, just maybe, I would not have changed a thing.

My son stands at 17 on the cusp of adulthood. He's a good kid: caring, inquisitive, goofy. He's looking at the bright future of career, relationships, growth, and achievements—ready to go out into the world and claim it as his own, just as I did before him.

I think I know what the world has in store, and I would like to caution him not to make the same mistakes I did. The "Dad" (or is it the "Mom")

part of me also knows, however, that adversity builds
character and that, even if I warn him,
he's probably not going to pay
attention anyway.

So, here is this book of photos and
captions—for my son, and for all of
you, our readers—with the hope that
these life lessons will go down easier
with a little humor. I know these
lessons are true . . . because I've
lived most of them.

M. W. D.

IF I KNEW
THEN WHAT
I KNOW NOW...

I would have ordered take-out.

IF I KNEW
THEN WHAT
I KNOW NOW

I would have gotten the

inside scoop on things.

IF I
KNEW
THEN
WHAT I
KNOW
NOW...

I wouldn't have worried about bad hair days.

IF I KNEW THEN WHAT I KNOW NOW...

I would have bent over backwards for more people.

I would
have
gone on
more
blind dates.

IF I KNEW THEN
WHAT I KNOW NOW...

I would
have made
new friends
but kept
the old.

I would have made lemonade out of those lemons.

IF I KNEW THEN WHAT
I KNOW NOW...

I would
have
embraced
technology
sooner.

IF I KNEW THEN WHAT I KNOW NOW...

I would
have
been
more
laid
back.

IF I
KNEW
THEN
WHAT I
KNOW
NOW...

I wouldn't
have straddled
the fence.

I would
have
volunteered
more.

I would have
never questioned
a good thing.

I would have used more moisturizer.

IF I KNEW THEN
WHAT I KNOW
NOW...

I would have let the good times roll.

I would
have reached
new depths.

I would have insisted on more quiet time.

IF I KNEW THEN
WHAT I KNOW
NOW...

I would have brought less baggage.

I would
have known
that
sleep was
overrated.

IF I
KNEW
THEN
WHAT I
KNOW
NOW...

I would
have dressed
for success.

IF I KNEW THEN WHAT
I KNOW NOW...

I would
have taken
more
time out.

I would have hung in there when times were rough.

IF I KNEW THEN WHAT I KNOW NOW...

I would have worried less about my net income.

I would have kissed more frogs.

IF I KNEW THEN WHAT
I KNOW NOW...

I would
have colored
outside
the lines.

IF I KNEW THEN WHAT I KNOW NOW...

I would have showered more people with love.

IF I KNEW THEN
WHAT I KNOW
NOW...

I would have read the comics first.

IF I KNEW THEN
WHAT I KNOW NOW...

I would
have kept
my cool.

I would have
had my cake and
eaten it too.

IF I KNEW
THEN WHAT
I KNOW NOW...

I would have let my imagination soar.

I would
have
invested
in real
estate.

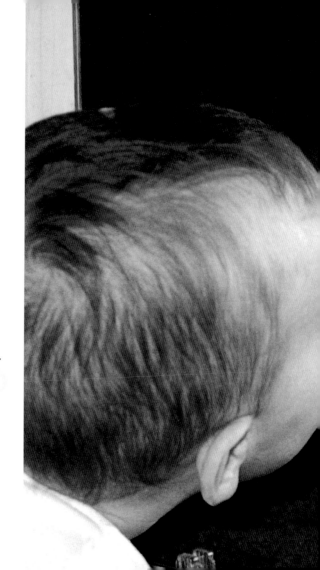

IF I KNEW
THEN WHAT
I KNOW NOW...

I would
have
improved
my self
image.

IF I KNEW
THEN WHAT
I KNOW
NOW...

I would have enhanced my star qualities.

IF I KNEW THEN
WHAT I KNOW NOW...

I would have remembered there's more than one fish in the sea.

IF I KNEW THEN WHAT
I KNOW NOW...

I would have stolen more kisses.

IF I KNEW THEN WHAT I KNOW NOW...

I would
have
traveled
in style.

IF I KNEW THEN WHAT

I KNOW NOW...

I would have been have been my own superhero.

IF I KNEW THEN
WHAT I KNOW NOW....

I would
have
looked
at things
from
all angles.

I would have given my compliments to the chef.

IF I KNEW
THEN WHAT
I KNOW NOW...

I would
have paid
closer
attention
to the
details.

I would have lived

in the moment.

PHOTO CREDITS